ANIMALS
Brightly Colored

Phyllis Limbacher Tildes

iⓘi Charlesbridge

My dazzling red feathers add a splash of color to a winter day, as I search for berries and seeds.

What am I?

a cardinal

Just as the winter snow
begins to melt, I look
for my mate.
Her feathers aren't as
bright as mine, but
she can echo my
cheery song:

*"What cheer,
cheer, cheer."*

I offer her my favorite
food—sunflower seeds.

I nibble on colorful coral in warm-water reefs. My bright blue scales blend in with my aqua world.

What am I?

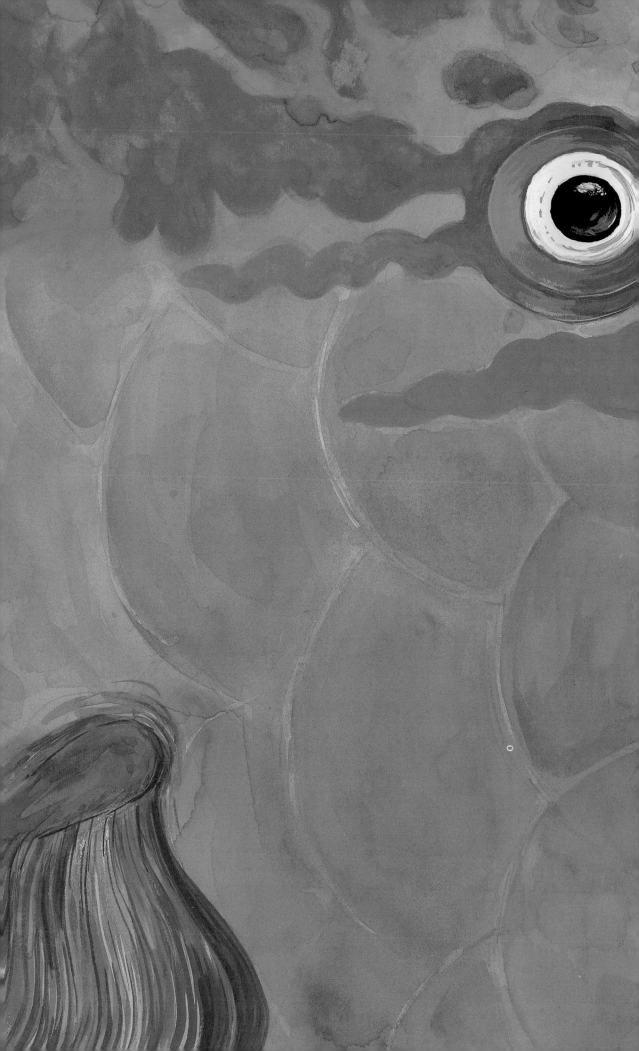

a parrotfish

Like the tropical bird,
I come in many colors.

With my bony mouth,
similar to a parrot's beak,
I crush and crunch the
hard coral. My dinner
crumbs become
fine beach sand.

I am not big,
but I am very
hairy and have
many feet.

I munch a bunch
of leaves for lunch.

What am I?

a caterpillar

I am a *yellow bear caterpillar.* I also like to eat cabbage and corn.

I make a soft cocoon and wait inside until I become a *Virginian tiger moth.*

I may look like a pretty plant with my pink belly, but I am an animal.

I have tentacles that sway in the currents of the sea.

What am I?

a sea anemone

With a stunning sting I zap and trap my prey, but my friends, the clownfish, can safely hide in my tentacles. In return, they chase away my enemies.

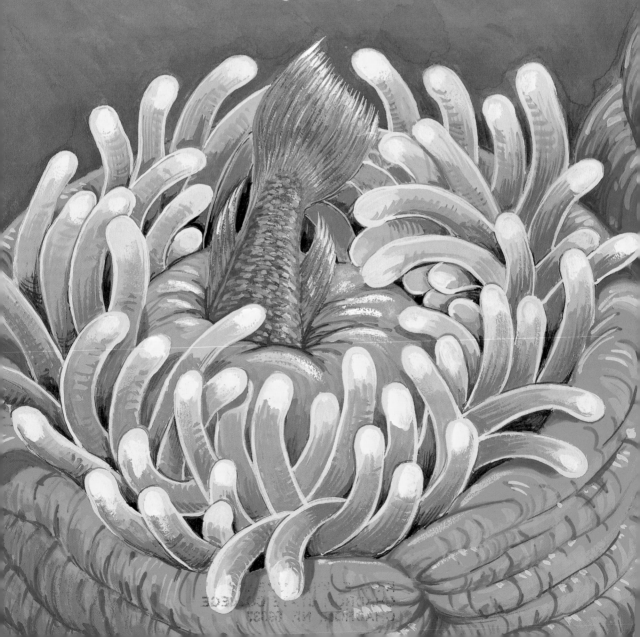

My elegant green scales sparkle like emerald jewels, but I have a reptile smile, long tail, and claws.

What am I?

an iguana

I am a very big lizard.
I like to lie on a sunny
branch of a tropical tree
after a lazy lunch of
leaves and fruit.

My fur is rusty orange. I am often called "sly," but I'm also quite shy.

I hunt for mice in the woods and fields at night.

What am I?

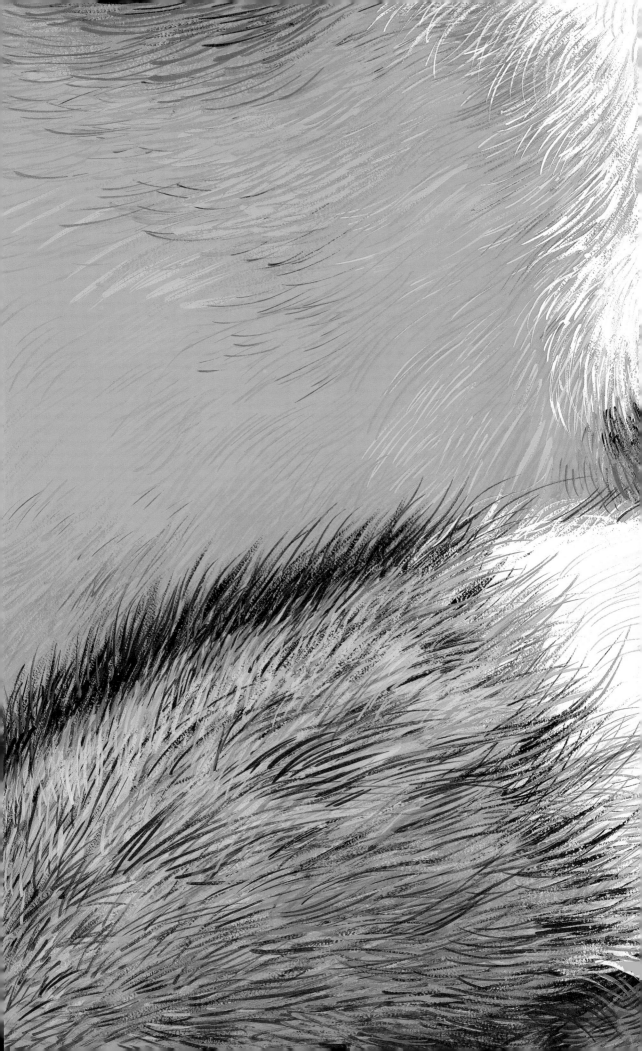

a fox

My mate and I make a cozy home for our pups in a hollow log, or we dig a den on a hidden hillside.

My brilliant feathers
flash in the rain
forest as I fly from
tree to tree
in search of
fruit and seeds.

I have a loud,
piercing call.

*What **am I?***

a macaw

I am the giant of the parrots. My large, powerful bill can crack a tough nut.

I am not only bright— I am smart, too!

Did you know?

The ***cardinal***, or redbird, as he is often called, is a resident of North America's woodlands, gardens, cities, and towns. With scolding cries and flapping wings, he fiercely defends his territory and mate. In fact, we rarely see this bright scarlet bird without his dull-colored partner. The female weaves a nest of bark, grass, small roots, and hair in a hidden thicket or dense shrubbery. The male feeds the female while she incubates three or four green-blue eggs. The busy father also feeds insects to his chicks when they hatch.

The ***queen parrotfish*** comes in many brilliant colors. It browses throughout the reefs in the tropical waters of the Caribbean and West Indies, feeding on algae that grows on a variety of plantlike animals called coral. It grinds up the coral using its "beak" and four teeth, which are set deep in its throat. It has a huge appetite and can grow up to four feet long and forty-five pounds. At night it can blow a clear protective bag around itself. Perhaps any movement against this bubble wakes the parrotfish and alerts it to possible danger. Many varieties of parrotfish can change their colors slightly to reflect their surroundings.

The ***yellow bear caterpillar*** has many yellow, white, orange, and reddish hairs on its body. These hairs are spiny and unappetizing to most predators. During the larva stage, the yellow bear caterpillar hatches from the eggs of a *Virginian tiger moth*. After it grows fat from feeding on lots of vegetation, it weaves a soft protective cocoon made from its own hairs. After a quiet rest in its pupa stage, it magically emerges as a moth from its cocoon with a yellow-striped abdomen and four white wings with small black spots.

A **sea anemone** is a deadly predator. Inside its beautiful plantlike tentacles is a poisonous stinger that stuns its prey. It feeds on small fish, plankton, and shrimp. Bright orange clownfish can hide in the anemone's tentacles because they have a slimy coating that protects them from the anemone's sting. The sea anemone has a sticky muscular "foot" that anchors it to rocks or other hard surfaces. It can even walk slowly across the ocean floor. Sometimes it somersaults or floats to move to a new location. Sea anemones can live up to one hundred years.

The **green iguana** lives in tropical South and Central America, Mexico, and the West Indies. This reptile can grow to be six to seven feet long and can weigh up to thirty pounds. The young iguana eats insects, but later prefers fruit, leaves, and flowers. An iguana is "voiceless" and has no communication by sound. To escape an enemy, it can leave a section of its tail behind or submerge itself under water for up to half an hour. Although it feels most secure in trees, the female iguana digs burrows in a sandy hillside to lay her eggs.

The **red fox** is not much bigger than a large house cat, and it weighs up to fifteen pounds. Like a cat, it pounces on its prey and has eyes with oval pupils, but the fox is actually a member of the dog family. The fox has unusually sensitive ears and often stands on its hind legs to hear better. Its diet consists of insects, rodents, birds, fruits, and acorns. The fox finds a mate in late winter. They dig a den that can be up to fifty feet long and has as many as five entrances and ten exits. Soon they have four to eight lively pups. Both parents will risk their lives to defend their pups from bears, dogs, wolves, owls, and other predators.

The plumage of the **scarlet macaw** is a startling rainbow of colors. Unlike many other birds, both the male and female share this bright plumage. Macaws live in the wet lowland forests of Mexico and Central and South America. They nest in cavities of dead palm trees as high as one hundred feet off the ground. After mating, the female macaw sits on her two eggs, while the male brings her food. Family members preen each other and chatter constantly with their larger social group. Macaws rest during the day and fly out together to feed in late afternoon, maneuvering gracefully between the branches of the rain forest canopy.

*For my brother, Doug,
with love*

With special thanks to my editor, Juliana McIntyre
— P. L. T.

Published by Charlesbridge Publishing
85 Main Street, Watertown, MA 02172-4411
(617) 926-0329
www.charlesbridge.com

Library of Congress Cataloging-in-Publication Data
Tildes, Phyllis Limbacher.
Animals: brightly colored/Phyllis Limbacher Tildes.
p. cm.
ISBN 0-88106-977-9 (reinforced for library use)
ISBN 0-88106-978-7 (softcover)
Summary: Presents specific information as clues to the identity
of various brightly colored animals, followed by the revelation of
the animals themselves.
1. Color of animals—Juvenile literature.
2. Animals—Identification—Juvenile literature.
[1. Animals.] I. Title.
QL767.T45 1998
591.47'2—dc21   96-47047

Printed in the United States of America
(hc) 10 9 8 7 6 5 4 3 2 1
(sc) 10 9 8 7 6 5 4 3 2 1

The illustrations in this book were done in gouache on
Strathmore 4-ply illustration paper, kid finish.
The display type and text type were set in
Impact and Veljovik by Diane M. Earley.
Color separations were made by Pure Imaging, Watertown, Massachusetts.
Printed and bound by Worzalla Publishing Company, Stevens Point, Wisconsin
This book was printed on recycled paper.
Production supervision by Brian G. Walker
Designed by Phyllis Limbacher Tildes